j          Collins, Kathleen.

            Sojourner Truth.

$21.25

| DATE | | | |
|---|---|---|---|
| | | | |
| | | | |
| | | | |
| | | | |
| | | | |
| | | | |
| | | | |
| | | | |
| | | | |
| | | | |
| | | | |
| | | | |

**PRIMARY SOURCES OF**
**FAMOUS PEOPLE IN AMERICAN HISTORY**™

# SOJOURNER TRUTH

## EQUAL RIGHTS ADVOCATE
## DEFENSORA DE LOS DERECHOS CIVILES

KATHLEEN COLLINS

TRADUCCIÓN AL ESPAÑOL:
EIDA DE LA VEGA

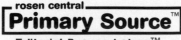

rosen central
**Primary Source**™
Editorial Buenas Letras™

The Rosen Publishing Group, Inc., New York

Published in 2004 by The Rosen Publishing Group, Inc.
29 East 21st Street, New York, NY 10010

**First Bilingual Edition 2004**
First English Edition 2004

**Cataloging Data**

Collins, Kathleen.
[Sojourner Truth. Bilingual]
Sojourner Truth: Equal rights advocate / by Kathleen Collins. — 1st ed.
    p. cm. — (Primary sources of famous people in American history)
Summary: Surveys the life of Sojourner Truth, who escaped from slavery and became famous as an advocate of equal rights for women and blacks.
Includes bibliographical references (p.  ) and index.
ISBN 0-8239-4169-8 (lib. bdg.)
1. Truth, Sojourner, d. 1883—Juvenile literature. 2. African American abolitionists—Biography—Juvenile literature. 3. African American women—Biography—Juvenile literature. 4. Abolitionists—United States—Biography—Juvenile literature. 5. Social reformers—United States—Biography—Juvenile literature. [1. Truth, Sojourner, d. 1883. 2. Abolitionists. 3. Reformers. 4. African Americans—Biography. 5. Women—Biography. 6. Spanish Language Materials—Bilingual]
I. Title. II. Series: Primary sources of famous people in American History (New York, N.Y.)
E185.97.T8C655 2004
305.5'67'092—dc21

*Manufactured in the United States of America*

**Photo credits**: cover pp. 5, 23, 27 (bottom), 29 courtesy of the archives of the Historical Society of Battle Creek; pp. 7, 21 Hulton/Archive/Getty Images; p. 9 Map Division, The New York Public Library, Astor, Lenox, and Tilden Foundations; p. 11 Picture Collection, The Branch Libraries, The New York Public Library, Astor, Lenox and Tilden Foundations; p. 13 Eastman Johnson, *A Ride for Liberty-The Fugitive Slaves*, 1863, Collection of the Brooklyn Museum of Art, 40.59a; pp. 15, 17 courtesy of the Phelps Stokes Collection, Miriam and Ira D. Wallach Division of Art, Prints, and Photographs, The New York Public Library, Astor, Lenox and Tilden Foundations; p. 19 Library of Congress Geography and Map Division; p. 25 Library of Congress Rare Book and Special Collections Division; p. 27 (top) National Portrait Gallery/Smithsonian Institution/Art Resource, NY.

Designer: Thomas Forget; Photo Researcher: Rebecca Anguin-Cohen

# CONTENTS

# CONTENIDO

# 1 BORN INTO SLAVERY

Sojourner Truth was born in 1797 in Ulster County, New York. Her given name was Isabella. She and her parents were slaves. Johannes Hardenbergh owned the family. Hardenbergh was Dutch and a wealthy landowner. Isabella's father was James Bomefree. Her mother was Betsey. The family's first language was Dutch.

---

# 1 NACIDA EN LA ESCLAVITUD

Sojourner Truth nació en 1797, en el condado de Ulster, Nueva York. La llamaron Isabella. Ella y sus padres eran esclavos. Eran propiedad de Johannes Hardenbergh, un próspero terrateniente holandés. El padre de Isabella era James Bomefree. Su madre se llamaba Betsey. El primer idioma de la familia era el holandés.

Sojourner Truth grew up with the name Isabella.

Sojourner Truth se llamaba Isabella.

Isabella was the youngest of 12 children. Her brothers and sisters were sold or given away before she was born. Isabella knew only one of her brothers, Peter. She knew that her parents were very sad about the loss of their other children. This sad feeling stayed with Isabella, too.

---

Isabella era la más joven de 12 hermanos. Sus hermanos y hermanas fueron vendidos o regalados antes de que ella naciera. Isabella sólo conoció a uno de ellos, Peter. Ella sabía que sus padres estaban muy tristes por haber perdido a sus hijos. Isabella también albergaba esta tristeza.

Slave markets like this one sold people at auction.

Los mercados de esclavos, como éste, subastaban personas.

## 2 SOLD FROM HER FAMILY

In 1808, Isabella was taken from her parents. She was sold to an English-speaking owner. She was sold several more times in her early life. From 1810 to 1827, she worked for John J. Dumont of New Paltz, New York. Isabella planted, plowed, and harvested crops. She also milked cows. In the house, she sewed, cooked, and cleaned.

---

## 2 SEPARADA DE SU FAMILIA

En 1808, Isabella fue separada de sus padres. La vendieron a un propietario de lengua inglesa. Fue vendida varias veces durante su juventud. De 1810 a 1827, trabajó para John J. Dumont de New Paltz, Nueva York. Isabella plantaba, araba y recogía las cosechas. También ordeñaba las vacas. En la casa, cosía, cocinaba y limpiaba.

This map of Ulster County, New York, shows many small towns. Slaves were often sold to nearby farms.

Este mapa del condado de Ulster, Nueva York, muestra muchos pueblos pequeños. Los esclavos eran vendidos con frecuencia a las granjas vecinas.

Dumont told Isabella she could go free in 1826. Later she hurt her hand. She was unable to work as hard as usual. Dumont felt he was cheated. He broke his promise. Isabella left with her baby anyway. Isabella later learned that Dumont had illegally sold her son, Peter. With the help of friends she sued Dumont. Peter was freed in 1828.

---

Dumont le prometió a Isabella que la liberaría en 1826. Pero cuando Isabella se hizo daño en la mano y no pudo trabajar como de costumbre, Dumont se sintió estafado y rompió su promesa. De cualquier modo, Isabella se marchó con su bebé, aunque supo más tarde que Dumont había vendido a su hijo Peter ilegalmente. Con la ayuda de amigos, Isabella demandó a Dumont y Peter fue liberado en 1828.

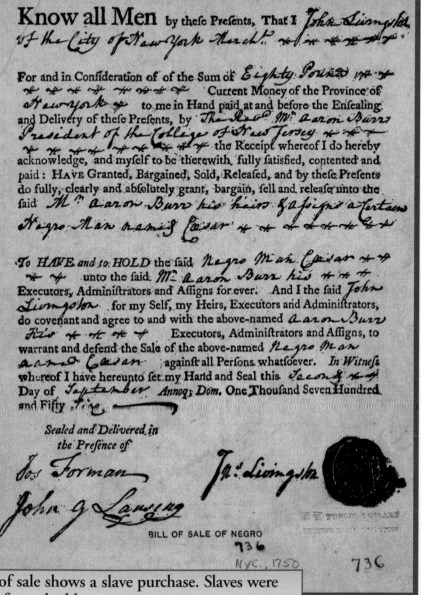

Know all Men by these Presents, That I John Livingston of the City of New York Merch.r

For and in Consideration of of the Sum of Eighty Pounds

Current Money of the Province of New york to me in Hand paid at and before the Ensealing and Delivery of these Presents, by The Rev.d Mr. aaron Burr President of the College of New Jersey the Receipt whereof I do hereby acknowledge, and myself to be therewith, fully satisfied, contented and paid: HAVE Granted, Bargained, Sold, Released, and by these Presents do fully, clearly and absolutely grant, bargain, sell and release unto the said Mr. aaron Burr his heirs & assigns a Certain Negro Man named Caesar

To HAVE and to HOLD the said Negro Man Caesar unto the said Mr. aaron Burr his Executors, Administrators and Assigns for ever. And I the said John Livingston for my Self, my Heirs, Executors and Administrators, do covenant and agree to and with the above-named aaron Burr his Executors, Administrators and Assigns, to warrant and defend the Sale of the above-named Negro Man named Caesar against all Persons whatsoever. In Witness whereof I have hereunto set my Hand and Seal this Second Day of September Annoq; Dom. One Thousand Seven Hundred and Fifty five

Sealed and Delivered in
the Presence of

Jos Forman
John G Lansing

Jn.o Livingston

BILL OF SALE OF NEGRO
736
NYC., 1750

736

This bill of sale shows a slave purchase. Slaves were thought of as valuable property.

Este comprobante muestra la compra de un esclavo. Los esclavos eran muy valiosos.

# 3 ESCAPE FROM SLAVERY

Isabella escaped from Dumont at the end of 1826. A friend told her to call on Isaac and Maria Van Wagener. The Van Wageners lived just a few miles down the road. They took in Isabella for the rest of her time as a slave.

The Van Wageners did not believe in slavery. Isabella and her baby, Sophia, lived with them for a year.

---

# 3 HUYENDO DE LA ESCLAVITUD

Isabella se fugó de casa de Dumont a fines de 1826. Un amigo le dijo que fuera a casa de Isaac y Maria Van Wagener. Los Van Wagener vivían a pocas millas de allí. Ellos cuidaron de Isabella hasta que dejó de ser esclava.

Los Van Wagener no creían en la esclavitud. Isabella y su bebé, Sophia, vivieron con ellos durante un año.

Sometimes slave families ran away from their owners. Most runaway slaves were caught and sent back to slavery.

Algunas veces, las familias de esclavos se escapaban de sus dueños. La mayoría de los esclavos fugados eran capturados.

In 1827, Isabella went to an African Dutch slave holiday celebration called Pinkster. There she had a powerful religious experience. Religion became an important part of her life from then on. For the rest of her life, she would hear voices and see visions. Her spirituality helped to keep her strong and brave.

En 1827, Isabella fue a una celebración de esclavos afroholandeses llamada Pinkster. Allí tuvo una poderosa experiencia religiosa. En adelante, la religión pasó a formar parte importante de su vida. El resto de sus días, Isabella oyó voces y tuvo visiones. Su espiritualidad la ayudó a mantenerse fuerte y valiente.

The English were not the only slaveholders in America. The Dutch took part in slavery, too.

Los ingleses no eran los únicos esclavistas de Estados Unidos. Los holandeses también lo eran.

Around 1829, Isabella moved to New York City. She took her two youngest children, Peter and Sophia, with her. Isabella met a wealthy social reformer named Elijah Pierson. She joined him in preaching in the streets.

Isabella could not read, but she was a very good speaker. She became well known for her preaching, praying, and singing.

———◆◆◆———

Alrededor de 1829, Isabella se mudó a la ciudad de Nueva York. Se llevó a sus dos hijos menores, Peter y Sophia. Isabella conoció a un próspero reformador social llamado Elijah Pierson. Juntos predicaron en las calles.

Isabella no sabía leer pero era muy buena oradora. Era muy conocida por sus sermones, sus oraciones y su canto.

**New York City in 1829. Here, Isabella found that she was a good street preacher.**

Nueva York, 1829. Isabella se dio cuenta de que era una buena predicadora callejera.

# 4 PREACHING FREEDOM

In 1843, Isabella decided to become a traveling preacher. She said that voices told her to sojourn the Northeast and Midwest. There she worked to speak God's truth.

To sojourn means to make short visits. Isabella changed her name to Sojourner Truth. From then on, she thought of June 1, 1843, as her birthday.

---

# 4 PREDICANDO LA LIBERTAD

En 1834, Isabella decidió convertirse en predicadora ambulante. Dijo que las voces le habían ordenado que viajara al Noreste y al Medio Oeste. Allí trabajó llevando la verdad de Dios.

"To sojourn", en inglés, significa hacer visitas cortas. "Truth", quiere decir verdad. Isabella se cambió el nombre a Sojourner Truth. A partir de ese momento, dijo que su cumpleaños era el 1 de junio de 1843.

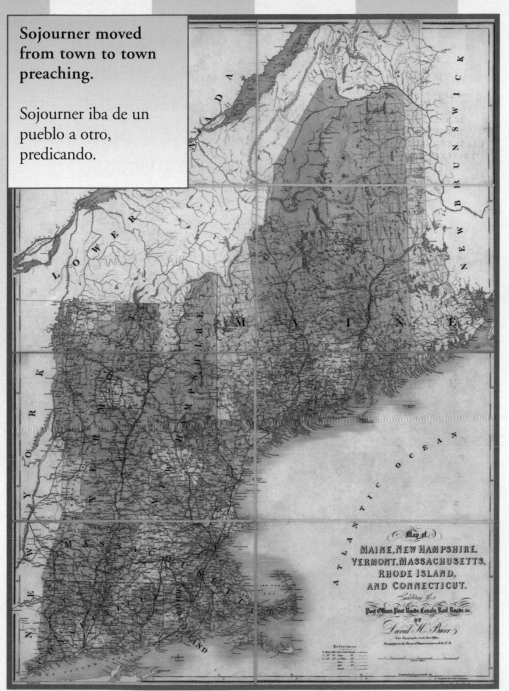

Sojourner moved from town to town preaching.

Sojourner iba de un pueblo a otro, predicando.

In the winter of 1844, Sojourner Truth moved to a commune in Massachusetts. It was called the Northampton Association for Education and Industry. There she met other members of the abolitionist (antislavery) movement. Abolitionism and women's rights became important to Sojourner Truth. She began to preach about these ideas, too.

En el invierno de 1844, Sojourner Truth se mudó a una comuna en Massachusetts. Se llamaba la Asociación de Northampton para la Educación y la Industria. Allí conoció a otros miembros del movimiento abolicionista, o en contra de la esclavitud. El abolicionismo y los derechos de las mujeres se convirtieron en temas importantes para Sojourner Truth, quien empezó a predicar estas ideas.

Abolitionists worked to end slavery all through the United States.

Los abolicionistas luchaban para acabar con la esclavitud en Estados Unidos.

In 1850, Sojourner published her autobiography. It was called *The Narrative of Sojourner Truth*. She sold it at women's rights meetings for 25 cents per copy. In 1851, she gave a speech in Ohio at the Akron Women's Rights Convention. She talked about being a slave. She talked about the sadness of having her own children sold.

En 1850, Sojourner publicó su autobiografía titulada *La historia de Sojourner Truth*. La vendía en reuniones sobre los derechos de la mujer a 25 centavos por ejemplar. En 1851, pronunció un discurso en la Convención de los Derechos de las Mujeres en Akron, Ohio. Habló de la esclavitud. Habló de la tristeza que siente una madre cuando sus hijos son vendidos.

NARRATIVE

OF

SOJOURNER TRUTH;

A Bondswoman of Olden Time,

EMANCIPATED BY THE NEW YORK LEGISLATURE IN THE EARLY
PART OF THE PRESENT CENTURY;

WITH A HISTORY OF HER

Labors and Correspondence,

DRAWN FROM HER

"BOOK OF LIFE."

BOSTON:
PUBLISHED FOR THE AUTHOR.
1875

SOJOURNER TRUTH,
"THE LIBYAN SIBYL."

**Sojourner Truth's life story told of her early pains as a slave.**

*La historia de Sojourner Truth* cuenta sus primeros sufrimientos como esclava.

# 5 WORKING TO END SLAVERY

In the mid-1850s, Sojourner moved to Battle Creek, Michigan. This was an important place for the antislavery movement. She helped freed slaves find jobs. She helped Michigan's black army soldiers. She worked to allow blacks to travel with whites on streetcars in Washington, D.C.

---

# 5 ACABANDO CON LA ESCLAVITUD

A mitad de la década de 1850, Sojourner se mudó a Battle Creek, Michigan. Éste era un lugar importante para el movimiento abolicionista. Sojourner ayudaba a los esclavos liberados a encontrar trabajo, ayudaba a los soldados del ejército negro de Michigan, y luchaba por que permitieran a los negros viajar con los blancos en los tranvías de Washington, D.C.

The abolitionist movement grew quickly during the Civil War. Abraham Lincoln freed the slaves in 1863.

El movimiento abolicionista creció rápidamente durante la Guerra Civil. Abraham Lincoln liberó a los esclavos en 1863.

In 1864, she met with President Abraham
Lincoln at the White House. In 1870,
Sojourner sent a petition to Congress. In it
she asked the government to give land in the
West to former slaves. Congress did not do
anything for former slaves. Sojourner
inspired thousands of former slaves to settle
their homes in Kansas.

En 1864, Sojourner conoció al presidente
Abraham Lincoln en la Casa Blanca. En 1870,
envió una petición al Congreso en la que pedía al
gobierno que le diera tierras en el Oeste a los
antiguos esclavos. El Congreso no hizo nada por
los esclavos liberados, pero Sojourner inspiró a
miles de esclavos liberados para que se asentaran
en Kansas.

Lincoln (*left*) met with many black abolitionists. Sojourner was well known to him. He signed her autograph book (*below*).

Lincoln (izquierda) se encontró con muchos abolicionistas. Lincoln había oído hablar de Sojourner antes de conocerla. Lincoln firmó su libro de autógrafos (abajo).

For Aunty
Sojourner Truth

A. Lincoln

Oct. 29. 1864

Sojourner continued to travel and speak in the 1870s. She talked about a homeland for blacks in the West. She gave speeches about equal rights for women and blacks. She died on November 26, 1883. In 1986, Sojourner Truth was honored on a U.S. postage stamp.

Sojourner continuó viajando y predicando en la década de 1870. Hablaba de una patria para los negros en el Oeste. Daba discursos acerca de la igualdad de derechos de las mujeres y de los negros. Murió el 26 de noviembre de 1883. En 1986, Sojourner Truth fue honrada con un sello postal.

Sojourner Truth's tombstone marks the resting place of this American hero.

La tumba de Sojourner Truth marca el lugar de descanso de esta heroína estadounidense.

# TIMELINE

1797—Isabella is born into slavery in Ulster County, New York.

July 4, 1827—New York State abolishes slavery.

1826—Isabella escapes to freedom with her infant daughter, Sophia.

1843—At age 46, Isabella adopts the name Sojourner Truth.

1850—Sojourner Truth publishes her autobiography.

1870—Sojourner sends a petition to Congress asking the government for a black homeland.

1883—Sojourner Truth dies in Battle Creek, Michigan.

# CRONOLOGÍA

1797—Isabella nace esclava en el condado de Ulster, Nueva York.

4 de julio de 1827—El estado de Nueva York abole la esclavitud.

1826—Isabella se fuga con Sophia, su hija pequeña.

1843—A la edad de 46 años, Isabella adopta el nombre de Sojourner Truth.

1850—Sojourner Truth publica su autobiografía.

1870—Sojourner envía una petición al Congreso pidiéndole al gobierno una patria para los negros.

1883—Muere Sojourner Truth en Battle Creek, Michigan.

# GLOSSARY

**abolitionist (a-buh-LIH-shun-ist)** Someone who works to end slavery.

**commune (KAH-myoon)** A community in which everyone shares similar ideas and is treated fairly.

**inspire (in-SPYR)** To fill with excitement about something.

**right (RYT)** Something that everyone should be able to have or do.

**slave (SLAYV)** Someone who is "owned" by another and does unpaid work for them.

## WEB SITES

Due to the changing nature of Internet links, the Rosen Publishing Group, Inc., has developed an online list of Web sites related to the subject of this book. This site is updated regularly. Please use this link to access the list:

http://www.rosenlinks.com/fpah/stru

---

# GLOSARIO

**abolicionista (el, la)** Alguien que lucha por que se termine la esclavitud.

**comuna (la)** Una comunidad en la cual todos comparten ideas similares y son tratados de manera justa.

**derecho (el)** Algo que todos deben tener la posibilidad de tener o hacer.

**esclavo(-a)** Alguien que es "poseído" por otra persona y hace trabajo no pagado para esa persona.

**inspirar(se)** Llenarse de emoción acerca de algo.

## SITIOS WEB

Debido a las constantes modificaciones en los sitios de Internet, Rosen Publishing Group, Inc., ha desarrollado un listado de sitios Web relacionados con el tema de este libro. Este sitio se actualiza con regularidad. Por favor, usa este enlace para acceder a la lista:

http://www.rosenlinks.com/fpah/stru

# INDEX

## ABOUT THE AUTHOR

Kathleen Collins is a writer living in New York City.

## ÍNDICE

## ACERCA DEL AUTOR

Kathleen Collins es escritora. Kathleen vive en la ciudad de Nueva York.